THE SALMON LEAP FOR PHDS

Swimming upstream: A transition
from academia to industry

The Salmon Leap for PhDs
Copyright © 2020 by Matteo Tardelli,
All rights reserved.

ISBN: 9798681267966

Disclaimer
All the material contained in this book is for educational and informational purposes only. The author of this book accepts no responsibility for any results or outcomes resulting from the use of this material. While every attempt has been made to provide information that is both accurate and effective, the author does

Copy editing by Eleanor Updegraff

Illustrations by Georg Liebergesell

MATTEO TARDELLI

To all my scientist friends

INTRODUCTION TO CAREER-HOPPING CREATURES

After ten years of working in academic research, I finally decided it was the right time for me to leave and, like a salmon, swim upstream on my career journey! I suddenly felt I was not exploring my full potential and had better skills to offer, and I didn't want to spend my career stuck in an ivory tower running western blots. Don't get me wrong: I loved my time there, and I loved the freedom and curiosity I could apply to my everyday job, but after a while it felt as if that path was leading nowhere.

Just like a salmon, I was born in fresh water and started my career in a private pharmacy in London right after my Masters degree. After living and working there for some time, I realized that I wanted more education and made my way out to the sea of academia, where I initially spent four years. I then embarked on postdoctoral training for another six years in different labs overseas. I slowly came to realize that academia – just like the open sea – is full of sharks and other predators waiting for you to make the wrong move. Not a good place to obtain job security, generally speaking. It is, however, a comfy spot to grow older in, gain priceless skills and create meaningful friendships.

After a few years, I'd gained significant experience, publications and techniques, but had also realized that there weren't many possibilities in the sea (there are few tenure track positions and far too many fish). The best option for me seemed to be to return to the private sector and battle my way upstream. That's why I decided to start this journey, leaping upstream through torrents and waterfalls, even though it felt like very hard work after spending so long in the relative comfort of the sea.

I thought making the transition from academia to industry was going to be as easy as finding another job, but slowly realized that wasn't the case! In fact, I was applying to jobs tirelessly every day and all I was getting in return were rejections. Clearly I was initiating my transition with the wrong steps: not investing enough time in understanding what I really wanted to do and crafting my application materials accordingly.

However, I wouldn't realize what I was doing wrong until much later, because nobody ever explained to me how to apply to industry jobs or make myself attractive after so many years stagnating in academic research. I also noticed that the topic of transition itself always felt like a taboo subject among my colleagues and supervisors. Something that you wouldn't discuss out loud.

On the one hand, I often got told that the value of a PhD is well recognized far beyond academia in terms of transferable skills, professional acumen, specialized knowledge, resilience and raw/analytical intelligence . Needless to say, numbers show[1] that increasing numbers of PhDs are making an impact across several disciplines and intramural institutions such as regulatory bodies, government, start-ups, industry and research. On the other hand, I also realized that what academia was offering to PhD holders was a lot of insecurity and imposter syndrome. In other words, that famous feeling of believing that you aren't as competent as others perceive you to be, which was slowly but incessantly growing in me.

Indeed, I found out that this pattern of insecurity was very common amongst my peers as the transition to private became such a huge topic of discussion within the PhD community. It was because it takes time and effort to build back our confidence after so many years of the 'you do not know enough' feeling, and nobody really coaches you on how to do this, or how to turn yourself into an attractive candidate for industry.

I figured out this concept whilst preparing my transition to industry after a relatively long career in academia – a time during which plenty of questions arose! In fact, looking at job vacancies advertised in the private sector puzzled me deeply. I wasn't even entirely sure what those complex titles really meant (Quality Control Scientist, Medical Science Liaison, Medical Manager, Field Application Scientist, Scientist II, Clinical Research Associate, etc.) because academia simply doesn't have as many!

The first step, then, was already hard enough: I needed to figure out precisely what to do whilst completely lost in this jungle of titles and acronyms. In addition, I was trying to understand which kinds of skills were really required (those buzzwords such as business acumen, team work, project management, etc.) that I perhaps should have built up far in advance before I started applying.

Not knowing where to go (or rather, swim) I found myself at a career crossroads. It felt unstable, uncertain, and extremely terrifying. I was sure to have a wide range of opportunities with my experience and degree, but where to go? What to do? How would I really know whether I was done with my postdoc and academia for good? I had to decide which direction to take.

Like a salmon leaping up rapids and waterfalls, I discovered that I needed to be intentional about my career and know where I was headed, even though I didn't know exactly what was waiting for me upstream.

On this journey, I had to face many expectations – first my own (I really wanted to become a professor) – and then of my family, boss, and peers. All of them told me different things, but most of all not to quit since I'd already come this far. But in the end, I found that closing some doors was OK! Ultimately, they weren't leading where I wanted to go.

I figured out that sharing this complex journey with you would benefit both of us, and so I created this book as a reference to prepare ourselves with. I gathered plenty of useful information from career coaches, careers fairs, and interviews with professionals who have managed a very successful transition. This is not meant to be another academic paper, but rather an operational manual laid out in a step-by-step and actionable fashion.

The backbone of this book is made up of eight perfectly balanced and information-packed chapters, of which the first four sum up advice for the exploration phase, while the last four dig deep into the action of job hunting. Although I've tried to rationalize them in a coherent flow, those steps are extremely interconnected and don't always come in chronological order.

This book will help you with:

- Showing the best side of yourself to potential recruiters by crafting your best possible resume and LinkedIn presence.

- Recognizing and managing negative feelings connected to the job hunt – before you end up smoked on a bagel (which is the sad fate of many salmon).

- Understanding the private-sector job landscape and hopefully having fun while doing it!

- Developing much-needed skills for the job market.

Now, let's get down to it and shape a career path you can be proud of!

CHAPTER 1

Work on yourself first! Self-assessment & introspection

"Knowing yourself is the beginning of all wisdom." – Aristotle

What do you believe you are good at? What are your top interests? What are your key values in life and work? These are all questions you should be asking yourself in an assessment phase. You'll need these answers to pinpoint the best career options later on.

But what exactly do I mean by values?

Values are beliefs about what is really important in your life that often align with your character and personality. When your values line up with your work and life, you feel more confident, valued and satisfied. Needless to say, working or living in ways that go against your personal values may lead to frustration, dissatisfaction and general discouragement, as you feel you aren't doing the right thing for yourself and the people around you.

It is therefore a very important first step to clarify your values and seek to match them to your work culture and potential new positions. For instance, some things that are vital for me are: helping others, having variety and challenges at work, getting paid well, and being autonomous. For you, it could well be that it's more important to be close to your family than to live in a big city, or to have a chilled life but still collect a big paycheck! There is no one-size-fits-all approach here.

In order to identify your own work values, you want to leverage the expertise you patiently built up in academia and channel this into a satisfying and meaningful career. A tool created by some big guys in the field – namely the Federation of American Societies for Experimental Biology (FASEB) and AAAS/Science – can help you with that. This web-based tool is called MyIDP (My Individual Development Plan) and is a well-designed career-planning tool tailored to meet the needs of PhDs and postdocs in the sciences. It is free to use and gives you a great starting point, asking you a bunch of questions that you're supposed to grade by numeric importance (give it a try at: https://myidp.sciencecareers.org/).

Equally important is asking people in real life, such as friends and family, what they believe you are good at, in order for you to critically assess and identify strengths based on their feedback. It's advisable to add a playful twist to this process to make it more interesting for you and others.

For instance, I recently discovered a new playful way of exploring values and understanding what other people see from the outside while learning more about myself too. With friends, I played the card game "We're Not Really Strangers", which brands itself as a purpose-driven card game all about empowering meaningful connections[2]. The game unfolds over three levels of questions and wildcards, starting with a perception phase before going deeper into connection and reflection. There is also a jolly card that you can only play once, which prompts your chosen player to explain and articulate more about a question (preferably an interesting or very embarrassing one!). I found this extremely useful and a good prompt for self-reflection, and I recommend you to try it out or explore other playful tricks to approaching difficult and personal questions. They're normally very tedious to answer, I know, but they will make your job hunting more focused and effective.

Typically in academia we tend to develop imposter syndrome and become insecure about ourselves, so working on your own confidence is pivotal as a starting point. Frankly, overcoming and caging the so-called "confidence Gremlins"[3] has been the most difficult part for me. I'm learning about this from the book *The Squiggly Career* by Helen Tupper and Sarah Ellis.

Gremlins constantly make you insecure through the professional use of unsolicited reminders such as, "See, you got your tenth rejection this month, you obviously aren't good enough!" In addition, they prevent people from getting out of their comfort zone and safe place, making you highly resistant to change. Telling these ugly (yet cute) devils, "GET OUT OF MY WAY!" was extremely difficult, yet the first trigger for a career change. It kept the door propped open, allowing me to creep outside my confidence bubble and start getting to know other people, different career stories and new possible avenues for myself, both as a person and as a professional.

I honestly find resources and communities such as PhD Balance (https://www.phdbalance.com/), created by Susanna L. Harris, great places where people can share their struggles and build back their self-confidence. As data suggests, almost half of PhD and graduate students struggle very much to maintain their mental health[4]. Sharing your story with like-minded people in a safe place can therefore be a great help.

Other questions to consider are: how do you keep yourself curious and growing while job hunting? Do you give yourself constant feedback during this upstream journey? The key is to keep learning and investing in yourself along the way, by:

- Acknowledging the fact that it is OK to change direction

- Making career development a real priority

- Surrounding yourself with the right people

- Seeking out professional help and career coaches that can help to shape your journey

Framing preferences, and better defining values and skills that align with potential employers are the next very important steps that you should consider taking.

Chapter Summary: Identify your work values as an essential piece of the career-planning puzzle! Take value-assessment and personality tests, talk to people and be introspective to reach satisfaction in your next job.

CHAPTER 2

Network: build it before you need it

"Networking is a lot like nutrition and fitness: we know what to do, the hard part is making it a top priority." – Herminia Ibarra

A network is your greatest ticket to a new career, as many job posts within your field might not be advertised. So how do you get to know about their existence? Through people! And you probably have more interesting connections in your network than you realize. Make sure they all know you are actively looking into new opportunities – this might drive referrals in the near future.

If that isn't enough and you feel you need to expand your boundaries, there are many places you can visit or activities you can do to expand your network. Alumni networks are also key to a successful search – in fact, most universities have alumni groups. Find out about people who graduated from your institution in the past ten years by looking them up on LinkedIn. The best sources of advice for PhDs moving from academic to non-academic work are people who have made the transition themselves. Alumni are easy contacts to make because you share something in common and they are sympathetic to your cause. They've been there themselves!

What does your network look like right now?

Personal: people outside your professional life (a friend of your dad's, that guy you met at someone's BBQ party, a cousin of your brother-in-law)

Professional: people who can help you get work done (colleagues, co-workers, actual and former bosses)

Mentors: people who can help with shaping your future goals (a person working in a position that you would love to have in the future)

In addition, it is very important to pay attention to opportunities around you through the savvy use of social media such as LinkedIn, Twitter and blogging. However, do make sure to have control over what's out there about you at first (as your prospective employer will most likely Google your name).

A practical list of actions aimed at expanding your network might look as follows:

1. **Set up an initial goal for the amount of people you are willing to meet this week** – whether that's happening over a coffee, at the postdocs social hour or at a careers fair is up to you.
2. **Plan to go to as many networking or career-developing events as you can**, perhaps reaching out to interesting people in advance (also planning some questions to ask once you meet). When you reach the event (well on time) showcase open and positive body language, smiling and looking people in the eye whenever it feels appropriate.
3. **Network one-to-one and not in groups**, making sure to always be an active listener! If after a couple of chats you

feel exhausted, take a break, go to the toilet or get some fresh air, recharge, and then get back in the room.

4. After the event finishes, **make sure to have contact details of interesting people to follow up with,** thanking them for their time and asking to keep in touch.

5. **Diving into alumni organizations, volunteering or professional societies** are great ways to get to know people. In fact, these groups can connect you with others that in turn might have information about jobs you actually want.

As a rule of thumb, people that you get to know in your personal life are the ones that probably will help you the most in finding a job. Meet people with similar but also different interests! That means, it's good practice to also attend events that are outside your expertise bubble to craft diverse connections and build your network quickly (making the process perhaps even more interesting and fun).

So, to recap: What makes a good networker? According to an article published on the popular website entrepreneur.com[5], seven characteristics make a great networker:

1. Good listener
2. Positive attitude
3. Collaborative (helps others)
4. Sincere and authentic
5. Follows up
6. Trustworthy
7. Approachable

The Hidden Job Market

Referrals might give you access to the hidden (or unadvertised) job market. But what is it exactly? These are all the jobs or potential jobs that are not formally advertised yet or still being created. For instance, one of your contacts might know that there is a specific person within the company who got promoted, is leaving or otherwise moving, creating a new job opening. This very contact might think about you and refer you for that position before it gets advertised.

As is widely recognized, companies value referral procedures very much as they prefer to hire candidates recommended by trusted people. Studies show that on average 250 to 300 applicants apply for each advertised job post, and only between two and five make it to the interview (in big companies)[6]. So skimming through those numbers is very time-consuming and cumbersome work for employers/HRs! Job seekers leveraging the hidden job market therefore have higher possibilities of getting an interview (as the vacancy isn't out there yet), and in fact up to 70% find their job through their network, it has been shown[6].

Try to think harder about some people in your network who know you, trust you, and can open doors for you (people you have worked with, family, friends, community members). Again, think of the people in your life who are connectors and who believe in you, reach out to them and let them know you are actively looking.

According to the website thebalancecareers.com[7], a few pieces of practical advice on how to tap the hidden job market could be:

- Network traditionally, but also by accepting invitations beyond traditional networking functions

- Volunteer with purpose at a company of interest

- Subscribe to Google alerts for the company you would like to work for, so as to get to know when they expand or open new offices (and are therefore hiring)

- Contact employers of interest

- Practice your elevator pitch

- Update your social networks with your new skills, so as to increase your visibility

Using Your Social Networks For Networking: Linkedin For Scientists

Let's face it: as scientists in academia and PhD holders we are often very bad at:

- Networking and getting out of our comfort bubble

- Marketing ourselves and being memorable

- Communicating our value

Which are all rather vital points in making individuals desirable and employable.

Here is where LinkedIn comes in handy.

LinkedIn is a medium rarely utilized by PhDs, who prefer instead to create a ResearchGate profile. However, although the latter is useful to get stats, readers and citations on your work, it doesn't help much if you're seeking new employment in the private sector.

Don't have LinkedIn yet? Here are some tips on how to build a successful LinkedIn for scientists profile and hopefully get recruiters to find you:

1. Forget about your stats and citations on ResearchGate and create a solid LinkedIn profile, completing all the sections so as to reach the most-wanted "All Star" status.

Be visible and open to connect!

2. Upload a nice, up-to-date and professional headshot – no pipettes, agarose gels, puppies or labmates, just you smiling with confidence at the camera! Your face should occupy about 60% of the circle.

3. Change the default background image to something demonstrating your area of expertise or aligning with your personal brand. Use online design tools such as canva.com to size exact dimensions (1584 x 396 pixels) and create pictures that are perfectly sized.

4. Write an impactful headline, with keywords highlighting your value in 1–2 job titles or areas you are interested in that align with the roles you would like to get. Make it interesting and differentiate from others – the goal is to get people to click on your profile and find out more about you! Don't forget to add your location too, or where you are looking into relocating to.

5. In the "About" section, put together a nicely spaced paragraph with key competencies in bullet points, adding contact details (so as to make it easier for people/ recruiters to get in touch with you). Use numbers to quantify your achievements, for instance "published 3 papers in *Nature*" or "won a grant for $400k of new research funding". People visiting your profile can only see the first three lines of this section before clicking to see more (and most people will not click through), so you need to get to the point quickly. The goal should be to have an interesting and compelling story here. Always write in the first person – "I am…".

6. The same applies to "Experience": spaced bullet points with relevant experience. Use the right keywords and phrases to come up in search engines for your industry, also making this section interesting and informative. As a general rule: describe the company you worked for and your role there in a couple of sentences , highlighting your main responsibilities and the value you can bring

to a new role if hired. I personally like to make things a bit more interesting by inserting thumbnails of my publications or relevant websites (spoiler – often LinkedIn doesn't work well with this function and things look a bit sloppy, so you'll need to find your way around it). Spaced paragraphs are meant to get people to scroll to the bottom of your profile, resulting in more time spent on it. In fact, it's well known that a high dwell time is rewarded by the platform and might drive increased search visibility.

7. Add your education at the bottom with thesis keywords. Make it as good as your CV!

8. Under accomplishments: don't forget to add publications. Again, it's a bit ugly-looking on LinkedIn – I know, but it's also a great idea to add collaborators (if they are on LinkedIn too). This might also increase dwell time.

9. Interact! Interact! Interact! – by posting, linking and commenting on other people's posts and generally speaking "adding value" to the platform. But most importantly: be consistent with it. In fact, commenting is a way to amplify your visibility and build relationships, and starting a meaningful conversation is the ultimate goal. This doesn't mean copying and pasting your newest publication's URL, but rather summing it up in paragraphs and making it intelligible to your audience (so they can interact with you), or writing what you are passionate about.

10. Overall, I believe that personal branding and storytelling needs a lot of attention here, as it makes opportunities coming your way (inbound) and networking simpler, giving you a purpose. Also, your top technical and transferable skills should be evident throughout your profile (again, a part of your personal branding). In fact, the idea is to build your profile as a trusted friend and a go-to expert. You aren't on LinkedIn

to sell something.

11. Lastly, remember that LinkedIn is a place to build relationships! Connect with people you talked to in real life, but if you wish to connect with a new person who could be interesting for your future career path, do so by adding a personal note briefly explaining why you'd like to connect. As always, keep it professional!

I know this takes time and effort, but you'll notice the difference in the first few weeks (if done right) as people interact with you more and more. My profile is far from being great, I must say, but by listening to experts like Kirsty Bonner and Maline Madine on their webinars, attending other seminars and endless Zoom calls, I am slowly getting an idea of how best to work with it.

Now that you know how to craft a very good-looking profile, you need the right industry people to view it, and that's where the right keywords and storytelling come into play! If you're impatient, please check Chapter 6 for more details.

Generally speaking, use these few seamless tricks to grow your network instantly:

- Import your mail contacts and send them a connection request

- Add all collaborators, former lab members, mentors and summer students

- Join LinkedIn groups that are interesting for you, participating in the conversation

- Check the business cards you might have from past events, and look for potential contacts to add to your online network

- Use the "people you may know" feature to find like-minded peers.

A Guide To Using Linkedin For Beginners

Having a good LinkedIn profile isn't enough – you need to know how to use the platform correctly too. So let's put theory into practice and use it to network!

These are some **common mistakes and things to avoid** in this process:

First and foremost: starting off with a vague message!Opening a professional relationship with a "Hey, how are you doing? I would like to add you to my network" kind of message will get you nowhere. Remember you are trying to connect (online) with a stranger here, so you need to add some value to the conversation, which will otherwise feel purposeless at first sight. Instead, get to the point by asking a quick, small, practical question you would like input on.

Asking something BIG right away. I know you would like to connect to ask this person a bunch of questions and perhaps even for a job. But you can't start like that. Instead, try to break things down a little into small and manageable questions, keeping in mind your ultimate goal. In the interest of saving time, try to focus on a small aspect of the advice you are really looking for (that perhaps can be answered in a few minutes), and explain why the other person is the best one to address that question. Mention here a bit of your background and context to add a personalized touch to the message. Very bad examples are "How do I find a job in your company?" or "What is the best strategy to get hired on LinkedIn?".

Expecting something in return without exchanging any value. Carefully check out and understand what this other person really cares about, and if there is any common interest that you can leverage or bring value to. A starting point could be sharing an article or a post that they care about, without asking for anything in return. By doing this, you'll show that your interest is genuine and that you care about building a real relationship. As in real life, building an authentic approach helps connect with people on a much deeper level!

Not following up. Always follow up with them after a couple of days, using a quick note to remind them about your message and show genuine appreciation for their time and energy.

Finally, make peace with the fact that you might not get a response back, even when you have the best intentions. Sometimes, people are just busy!

Chapter Summary: Create new connections and explore career options outside the lab! Implement networking in your everyday schedule, keeping a positive and open mindset. You want to come across as an interesting individual eager to enrich yourself with other people's experience.

CHAPTER 3

*Active research into potential
career paths and positions*

"Find out what you like doing best and get someone
to pay you for doing it." – Katherine Whitehorn

Unfortunately, (or rather, fortunately) there are no such things as self-driving careers. In fact, it's key to start doing your research and understand what roles are out there – classic questions to be answered here are: What options do you have? And what do you really want to do? This connects a lot with Chapter 1, as once you have established your values you can find companies and positions that satisfy the latter.

There are many options for PhDs other than linear progression to the academic life of a professor, but a common mistake is that we begin thinking about these different options way too late or only after finishing graduate school.

There are many paths out there that branch off the side of tenure track:

- Publishing

- Industry/Biotech

- Policy making

- Science communication/medical writing

- Journalism

- Consulting

- And many more popping up as you read...

It is critical to explore these alternative career paths while you're still a PhD student, but if you haven't looked into these options before (like I didn't), you can start now while thinking about your next challenge.

Studies show that doctoral students who don't do this are exposed to a narrow range of career opportunities[8-9]. A couple of solutions to this could be:

- Applying for an internship at a non-profit group or company, which can help you understand how to use your research skills in different ways.

- Considering volunteering by matching your volunteer interests with your academic areas of specialization: healthcare, economics, consulting or the environment. This will allow you to build networks outside of academia, add value to your skill set, and gain relevant work experience.

What can you do with your degree? Whether you completed a degree in computer science or molecular biology, you will have numerous career options to consider. Take some time to research different career paths related to your field before you make any major decisions. You can explore your options by:

- Conducting research online

- Speaking to people who work in the field you studied in

- Finding out what graduates who studied a similar degree have gone on to do

- Attending career events

Research occupational information

Once you have come up with a shortlist of occupations that you're interested in, it's a good idea to research occupational information to find out more details about them. Occupational information includes details about a particular job such as:

- Typical day: duties and responsibilities

- Personal requirements for people working in that occupation

- Related courses and professional associations

- Labour market information

- Similar occupations

Researching occupational information can help you make an informed decision about jobs you are interested in, rather than making decisions on what you think a job involves (which may be incomplete or inaccurate).

Research industry information

After identifying some occupations that are of interest to you, you can now look at which specific companies you would like to work for. Some questions to ask yourself could be:

- Are you keen on working within a specific field or industry (for example, government, pharma or the not-for-profit sector, established company or small start-up)?

- Or are you open to find out about opportunities across different industries?

Whichever way, there are a number of steps you can take to pinpoint your career options in several industry areas.

I would recommend starting by creating a preferred company list:

- Write down a list (or create an Excel sheet) of fifteen companies you would like to work for and are most interested in. This might be based on disease areas that align with your expertise, or product interest and/or the geographical area you would like to live in/relocate to.

- To this list, also add the names of scientists that work at that company and their contact information. It's very easy to connect with them on LinkedIn and keep up a meaningful conversation.

This will help you laser-focus your job search, start getting to know people and build a network within the company.

Find out about professional associations

Professional associations provide an enormous range of information and resources on a specific industry or professional area. Never underestimate their huge worth! You can find a professional or industry association for almost every area of employment, and most will offer career resources explaining how to thrive and develop a career in that area. Professional associations can provide valuable insight into the industry gold standards which are necessary for a newcomer to build a career in that area. The requirements for professional recognition or membership/subscription are also a useful tool for you to understand whether your degree and experience are competitive for that profession. Easy examples are: postdoctoral associations, Medical Science Liaisons association, career development association for scientists, STEM associations, etc.

Research career options using your sparkling new LinkedIn for scientists (Chapter 2)

You can use LinkedIn to research companies, industries and opportunities that relate to your degree.

If you have a shortlist of occupations or names of organizations that you are interested in, try searching for these in the "Advanced Search" option to see if anyone in your network works in these roles or companies. You can then connect with them to find out more about their jobs, industry or company by reading their LinkedIn profiles or arranging an informational interview (see Chapter 5).

If you don't have a particular occupation or company that you are interested in, or if you're trying to broaden your range of career options, you could start by simply typing your area of study or your interests as keywords into the "Advanced Search" tool. For example, if you are studying biology, but you aren't sure what kind of jobs exist related to biology, where they are and what kind of experience you need to get them, simply type "biology" into the "Keyword" box in LinkedIn's "Advanced Search" tool. LinkedIn will generate a list of anyone who has the word "biology" in their profile (though this might result in a very broad and general search). Click on the profiles that interest you and look for job titles that you might want to pursue, employers who hire people with these job titles, and the LinkedIn groups people belong to when they have similar interests to yours. You can get in touch with them and use informational interviews to research particular job roles and broaden your horizons.

Different career paths outside academia

While looking into industry positions, I quickly realized I had no understanding whatsoever of what those complex titles really meant. In addition, I wasn't sure whether I wanted to migrate into a completely non-bench kind of work. Especially because I had been doing bench and lab work for so long! Would I miss all this pipetting action someday? Thinking that many of you might feel the same, I decided to write a few words on shedding light on these complex buzz-worded titles.

So, without further ado, let's try to get some clarity! This section is divided into non-bench and bench-based positions as follows:

Non-Bench Positions

Product Manager: The Product Manager is responsible for managing the entire life cycle of a product. In this role you will have to monitor and adjust product strategies as new assumptions or market conditions arise. Therefore, along with a deep understanding of the technology itself, you should have a blend of business acumen, sales skills and understanding of the competitive landscape. You will act as the primary contact on product issues, maintaining, executing and creating plans and procedures for multiple products over local and regional sites, as well as collaborating with and supporting the sales team with forecasting monthly reports and sensitivity tracking.

Research Analyst in Venture Capital: The main responsibilities of a Research Analyst are to identify new investment opportunities, evaluate new inventions, and determine whether they will be worthy of investment. You will be required to map the product offerings of start-ups or companies against the broader competitive landscape, and screen potential investment opportunities via initial calls with company management (like CEOs or CFOs). You will have to develop a solid understanding of the technology and the company's pipeline (and the science behind it!), derived from in-depth research, and present the results to your managers. Practically, you will be creating data-backed support for investors in order for them to select the best possible investment opportunities. Scientific knowledge aside, you will be required to develop excellent networking and presentation skills, and have the ability to recognize the potential for commercial success in a new technology. This position is advisable for a people person, and not for someone who prefers to work alone or isn't comfortable with regularly meeting new people.

Consulting: As a Life Sciences Consultant you will be seen as a technical expert thanks to your PhD degree, however to be successful in this role you will need to develop new cutting-edge strategic and managerial skills as well. You will work collaboratively with peers and senior leadership to define initial hypotheses, researching markets and competitors, and also producing fact-based and analytically robust conclusions. You will basically apply the technical and scientific expertise that you built during your PhD to client issues. All the major consulting firms are hiring PhDs for their life science branch nowadays, with examples being LEK Consulting, Accenture, BCG, IQVIA, and Evercore. If you believe this could be an interesting path for you, I strongly recommend getting first-hand experience by applying for summer internships or for instance working/volunteering for PreScouter Inc. Prescouter is an American company which provides real-time solutions to clients by scouring the online market for innovative technologies of interest. They have a program called the "Global Scholar Program", in which they recruit freelance academics for different roles. Once registered, you will create your profile and be able to apply to projects based on your interests, working totally flexibly and remotely in exchange for a small compensation (isn't that cool?).

Scientific/Medical Writing: As a Science/Medical Writer, you will be asked to develop promotional and educational content for clients including slide decks, symposium and congress material, or other evidence-based documents (such as manuscripts, abstracts, posters, and clinical study reports). You should have a deep understanding of your assigned therapeutic or disease areas (which might well be your topic of scientific expertise), making sure deliverables are completed in a timely manner. In other words, as you previously performed for your PhD or postdoc, you will gather a large amount of information and then select what is more appropriate and suitable for your articles' (and clients') needs. You can find these kinds of positions at communication companies providing services to the pharmaceutical industry, or also within the pharma companies themselves! Do not confuse this role with a Medical Editor, who instead takes care of reviewing concepts, copy, layouts, and the final look of an existing document. They also edit grammar, spelling, punctuation, structure, and style, while verifying data and content too.

Life Science Business Development Manager: In this role you will be required to understand the value of the life science market opportunities for company products and expertise. You should be able to identify and scout new product (or derivative product) opportunities and prepare marketing justifications for their development, communicating these opportunities to management. You will facilitate and orchestrate the sales process from lead identification through close of sale. You will thus work closely with the sales support team to develop the appropriate solutions for clients. You will be expected to manage multiple projects and key industrial (but also academic) collaborators to develop new ideas, products and solutions for the life science market. You will be asked to travel for a good amount of your working hours, to attend and present key company advances, applications and solutions at scientific conferences.

Application Scientist, Field Application Scientist, Technical Support Scientist, or Field Support Scientist (many names meaning the same thing): This role is especially suitable for those who want to move away from repetitive bench work such as isolating RNA and pipetting your own rt-PCR, and rather dedicate themselves to more business-oriented roles. I believe this is an easy transitional position as you can still apply your technical and scientific knowledge related to a specific product or lab equipment. You will be required to meet new people and help them solve problems, so good communication skills and the ability to explain instructions in an uncomplicated and tangible fashion are definitely desirable skills to have. In detail, you will perform product demonstrations at customer or company sites, present seminars to a wide array of audiences, but also support and prepare technical training for in-house sales representatives. In a post-sale scenario, you will also provide troubleshooting support to customers in the field or by phone/email. Providing and continuously updating customer contacts with relevant information is also important, as well as tracking, recording and documenting all technical inquiries from customers.

With time, you will build a considerable network that will help you into new roles. In fact, the vast majority of application scientists move on to higher positions in other divisions such as business development or marketing. The frequent client interaction is the reason for the idea that the position of Field Application Scientist is the perfect transitional phase between lab and business work.

Research and Development (R&D) Project Manager: One of the main tasks of the R&D Manager is to lead/oversee processes and techniques used by the R&D scientists, making sure that financial support is being utilized properly. The ultimate aim here is to develop new products and processes that enable next-generation technologies. You will thus be building and leading strong multi-functional global teams of scientists and engineers dedicated to innovation in project execution. This role will ensure that the project you are overseeing is undertaken by the R&D team in alignment with the long-term strategy of the company. You will be managing your team, evaluating scientific data, and maintaining communication and collaboration with other divisions and academic entities that enable breakthrough innovation. I know many people who decided to take a project management certification to increase their chances of getting hired for this job. Although this might not be necessary, it could perhaps be an advantage to stand out in comparison to other candidates. Depending on the amount of time and money you want to spend on this certificate, you can find plenty of online courses from great universities and business schools.

Medical Science Liaison (MSL): The Medical Science Liaison (MSL) is part of a field-based team within the Medical Affairs Department and plays an important role in establishing, cultivating, and maintaining relationships with Key Thought Leaders (KTLs) in a specific therapeutic area. You will need to demonstrate the ability to interpret scientific data, communicate these to broad audiences, and understand the potential impact of the latter on clinical approaches and research needs. The MSL is responsible for leveraging his or her scientific background, industry knowledge, and business acumen to engage in appropriate communication with KTLs in an assigned territory regarding research activities, publications, education, consulting, and other Medical Affairs initiatives. Further, the MSL provides product and pipeline therapeutic area expertise to address KTLs and Healthcare Professional (HCP) inquiries and serve as a scientific expert to internal stakeholders. The biggest misconception regarding MSLs is that this is a sales position. Actually, MSLs are scientifically trained field personnel who are officially considered part of the medical staff. A good resource for information on how to break into this field are the websites: https://www.fromsciencetopharma.com/ and https://www.themsls.org/.

Regulatory Affairs: Since pharmaceutical companies are dealing with people's health, it goes without saying that they can be heavily regulated and big bureaucratic institutions to some extent. They therefore need whole departments taking care of this, and more specifically people maintaining knowledge of Good Clinical Practice (GCP), clinical research activities, and guidelines related to consent, ethical conduct and protection of human subjects. In this role, you will have to interact and assist regulatory specialists with obtaining continuing approvals from various committees and organizations (in-house: Scientific Committee, Institutional Review Board, Biosafety Committee, Radiation Committee, etc). You will have to assist and liaise with research nurses on administrative tasks as needed, as well as obtaining signatures on regulatory documents, filing study documents, processing personnel changes, revising regulatory documents and maintaining study binders/electronic folders. In other words, if you love paperwork and reading technical stuff, this is definitely the role for you!

Clinical Research Associate (CRA): Besides crunching regulations on drug development programs, companies also need people to contribute to the design of clinical trials and review trial documents. This is the Clinical Research Associate (CRA). As a CRA you will perform monitoring in the field, also communicating what is right and what's wrong to investigators and their staff. You will also have to perform on-site data verification/data integrity checks, assist site personnel with internal audits or regulatory inspections, track site performance and write follow-up visit reports. You will ensure compliance with the procedures to apply in the event of serious adverse events (common with any drugs) and draft an appropriate intervention plan for the avoidance of redundant errors and deviations. Many CRAs work remotely, which is a big plus if you are looking into becoming location-independent! From time to time you will be required to travel to the site where the trial you are overseeing is taking place. I personally know some colleagues who embarked on a Masters program in data management and trial coordination as they wanted to target this very position and grow within companies like Covance that offer global clinical development services.

Clinical Scientist: The Clinical Scientist function provides scientific expertise necessary to design and deliver clinical studies and programs. You will be responsible for the design and execution of assigned clinical trial activities and work closely with clinical team members within the assigned project to execute activities associated with the conducting of it. You may serve as Clinical Trial Lead for one or more trials, while supporting trial-level activities for one or more trials with the necessary supervision. You will collaborate and liaise with external partners (e.g. Key Thought Leaders), develop protocols and documents/ amendments, and present these to the governance committee and development team meetings as required. You will monitor clinical data for specific trends and develop data review plans in collaboration with Data Management.

CMC Scientist: CMC stands for Chemistry, Manufacturing and Controls. All stages of the drug development life cycle after drug discovery involve CMC. This position involves the critical evaluation of analytical data, knowledge of fundamental principles of organic chemistry and/or pharmaceutical sciences, and experience in drug product and drug substance CMC development. A successful candidate is expected to pay scrupulous attention to detail, to proactively identify key issues, to negotiate the delivery of approved technical documents in accordance with project timelines, and to respond to CMC development opportunities. As a CMC Scientist you will coordinate filing activities, compiling information from scientists and authoring the CMC sections of regulatory documents to support the timely submissions of both investigational and marketing applications of new drugs. Responsibilities also include coordinating the assembly of prompt and accurate technical responses to inquiries from the FDA and other regulatory agencies on the CMC sections of regulatory documents. These tasks will be performed in close collaboration with a bunch of other key departments such as Chemical & Synthetic Development, Drug Product Science and Technology, Analytical & Strategy Operations, Global Manufacturing, etc. A successful candidate will also be responsible for providing feedback to the Integrated Development Team on CMC issues and developing timelines for the completion of the CMC sections of regulatory documents.

Bench-Based Positions

Research & Development Scientist, Staff Scientist, Scientist I, R&D Specialist: The specific job titles may vary significantly, however they will always contain the word "Scientist" in one form or another – for instance, Senior Scientist, Staff Scientist, Scientist I or II (the number is proportionate to the level of experience), or R&D Scientist/Specialist. Principal Scientist is more of a PI position just within industry, so you must have relevant experience to apply to that. Generally speaking, the drug discovery process and preclinical research are perfect transitional jobs for PhDs leaping out of academia, as they comprise much of the expertise that you might already be very familiar with. As an R&D Scientist you will screen for potential therapeutic compounds and test their efficacy and safety in pre-clinical models. You will be experienced in handling and working with mice, as well as in general surgical techniques. As in your PhD, after the experimental endpoints are reached you will collect blood and tissue samples for further characterizations. You will be responsible for conducting the *in vitro* and *in vivo* experiments, predominantly for basic science, analyzing data and interpreting the results of experiments within the context of the research project goals. You will work closely with your supervisor to prepare and deliver effective oral presentations and papers in your area of expertise during internal and external meetings. Exactly as you might be doing right now, when things don't work you will troubleshoot why not and solve methodological or technical issues, interpreting experimental data and literature, and communicating results to the department or project team. Finally, you will collaborate and communicate efficiently with team members to coordinate complex *in vivo* experiments, and with other departments to facilitate cross-functional efforts.

Process Development Scientist – Downstream and Upstream: Process Development Scientists work in the later stages of research and development, and their efforts are mostly focused on optimizing the manufacturing process. This optimization can involve developing new machinery that may be necessary for scale-up or streamlining protocols, so an engineering background may be helpful for some positions. According to the stage of the manufacturing process you are working on, this position can be distinguished into upstream and downstream roles.

As a Scientist in Downstream Process Development, you will be responsible for conducting research and development that leads to efficient, scalable purification processes for therapeutic molecules. In this role you will develop and implement scalable purification processes for large molecule drug substances (e.g. monoclonal antibodies, fusion proteins, etc.) to meet established timelines, as well as designing and executing downstream process development laboratory studies. You will be asked to author electronic notebook records, process descriptions, process development reports, and other documentation/technical reports for the progression of assets and/or support of regulatory filings.

As a Scientist in Upstream Process Development, you will play a key role in supporting early project transitions between discovery/pre-clinical and process development functions. This might include routine cell culture laboratory work (shake flasks and bioreactors), cell culture media and feed optimization, process development and optimization. You will therefore perform hands-on bioreactor runs, support equipment maintenance, and provide other laboratory systems oversight, interfacing with analytical development to create robust early process and product characterization. This position might also involve lab-based experimental work (60–70% of the time) and project coordination within a cross-functional group of CMC scientists.

Just for clarity's sake: the upstream processing is a bioprocessing phase in which cell lines are generated, for instance a biomass is produced at an appreciable scale. The downstream processing phase deals more with the extraction or separation of desired products from the biomass previously developed in the upstream processing.

Manufacturing Scientist: In this role you will most likely be monitoring, controlling and improving the manufacturing processes of assigned products. You will be responsible for the planning, implementation and maintenance of manufacturing methods, processes and operations for current and new product lines, as well as contributing to the improvement of production capabilities. The Manufacturing Scientist is also responsible for understanding product specifications, troubleshooting technical problems, and implementing process improvements.

You will practically produce products, kits and reagents that meet product specifications and timelines. This involves accurately and completely recording production and in-process testing results in approved batch record forms and work order documents. You will also manage inventories, supplies and equipment in order to achieve production plans; assist in the review and validation of product development protocols, and in implementing these procedures through the use of approved written work instructions; assist in the maintenance and calibration of equipment that is used in production, using established or manufacturer-supplied procedures; and communicate production status to the Manufacturing Manager in a timely manner, including any operational issues.

Laboratory Manager, Laboratory Head: The Laboratory Manager/ Head is not necessarily a bench role, but a bit of a hybrid one. On the one hand, you will manage the operational activities of research laboratories and supervise a variety of activities related to the planning, performance and supervision of basic and/or clinical research. On the other hand, you might be asked to participate in new assay development, buffer preparations and test system validations. In addition, you might be asked to implement and enforce procedures to support laboratory safety, efficiency and quality control. I personally received orientation, training and supervision by a Lab Manager when I started my postdoctoral training in NYC, who instructed me on how to use new equipment as well as how to maintain and follow the standard operating procedures for laboratory activities. Other responsibilities may include maintaining an inventory of and ordering supplies, equipment and reagents; receiving supply orders and confirming accuracy of delivery; and negotiating prices with external vendors for reagent/equipment purchases. I see this role as a blend of technical, bench and operational work.

Quality Control Scientist: The Quality Control Scientist is responsible for supporting quality control bioanalytical testing for the release of clinical and commercial products. This includes the ability to interface with multiple groups, and the ability to independently perform tasks, interpret results and troubleshoot. Additionally, in this position you might be asked to assist with training and assay transfer. You will need advanced hands-on experience with various analytical techniques such as flow cytometry (highly dependent on the specific role) and scientific knowledge in the characterization and transfer of pharmaceutical products. An advanced ability to accurately and completely understand, follow, interpret and apply Global Regulatory and Current Good Manufacturing Practice (cGMP) requirements is also essential. You will be asked to communicate effectively with peers, department management and cross-functional peers, also demonstrating advanced technical writing skills.

If you made it this far you might be noticing that pharmaceutical and generally private industries are far more collaborative than academia. You will never take care of a single project by yourself, but always interface with other professionals towards a common goal! As you have just read above, there is a somewhat common pattern in the kind of skills required, and although job titles and responsibilities sound very different, certain soft skills are widely appreciated across all levels.

Just pick what you feel is the best fit for you and work towards landing that job!

Chapter Summary: Find out what your career options are, learn the real meaning of the job title you are applying for, and once you've found one (or more) that aligns with your values and career perspectives, craft your search around it.

CHAPTER 4

Identify skill gaps for a
successful transition

"Start by doing what is necessary, then what is possible, and
suddenly you are doing the impossible." – Francis of Assisi

The huge variety of career options available nowadays
can demand a diverse array of skills, such as being an
effective communicator, writing grant proposals and crafting
presentations to diverse audiences. The National Postdoctoral
Association (NPA) recently identified six core competencies[10] for
postdocs which are in high demand in the current job market:

1. Discipline-specific conceptual knowledge
2. Research skill development
3. Communication skills
4. Professionalism
5. Leadership and management skills
6. Responsible conduct of research

All these should be naturally outlined in your resume with
compelling real-life examples. In the process of gathering further
feedback from career coaches, trustworthy online resources and
career development offices, I found out that everyone aligns

themselves with this list. In fact, it seems that the top transferable skills for employers are still the very classic ones: communications, time management, collaboration, networking, leadership, and mentoring. And as PhDs, we have them all! But what do those words really mean?

Let's analyze some in detail:

Time management and organization: It is important to be exceptionally organized when managing your own individual responsibilities or your team's projects overall. For instance, in the pharmaceutical industry, large quantities of highly time-sensitive clinical data and regulatory submissions are generated daily. As such, time management is considered a crucial transferable skill for this sector and pharmaceutical hiring managers rigorously test candidates for it. Making effective use of available time on a daily basis and maintaining progress towards organizational goals is essential to your success in industry. **Example:** On some busy days I run several gels and rtPCRs simultaneously, while being just on time for the lab meeting presentation!

Information management: This means that you are able to filter through large amounts of research data and identify relevant trends. You must also understand that the key to successful information management in industry is not just gathering and understanding information, but is all about translating information into practical and actionable intelligence, therefore bringing value to the table. **Example:** I filtered through a bunch of results from a microarray data set and translated those apparently meaningless numbers into concise messages and future directions, which I made intelligible for my boss and peers.

Communication and client-facing skills: As we discovered earlier in Chapter 3, industry is far more collaborative than academia. In industry, you will be required to attend many more internal and (especially) external meetings than you are used to. This is why biotechnology and pharmaceutical companies carefully screen job candidates' personality traits during interviews. They want to know: Can he/she work well with our established team? Will he/she maintain her professionalism at all times? Will he/she be able to handle stress on a bad day? **Important to remember:** PhD candidates that have the required technical skills but lack certain personality traits will not get hired into industry roles. You should thus look into preparing very well for these kinds of questions, so as to convey your best side while interviewing. **Example:** I successfully collaborated and communicated with several international lab members, but also with other professionals such as sales reps, delivery personnel, research technicians and nurses.

Project management and strategic planning: Even if you aren't officially working as a project manager, you will need to know how to efficiently manage your own projects. Fortunately, that is exactly what you are currently doing every day in your PhD studies or postdoc (managing and planning experiments). You will need to know how to hit both timeline and budgeting goals. Most importantly, the purpose of your project in industry needs to reflect the company's long-term goals/objectives and increase profit. **Example:** I managed my own projects from planning through execution and troubleshooting each time I got assigned a new one during my PhD and postdoc.

Professional awareness and adaptability: Flexibility and professional awareness, though not technical, are critical skills in industry. You should be ready to thrive and adapt to a fast-paced environment, also being able and willing to drop a project after a few months if it's not promising. **Example:** Each time I changed labs, I had to adapt to my new colleagues, city, boss and projects very fast. I quickly got used to the new environment and started to ramp up experiments in the very first months.

Remember, industry organizations not only value your scientific knowledge and technical skills, but also your ability to transfer your non-technical skills to their culture and working environments overall.

If you hope to transition into a non-academic career, the time to start developing your transferable job skills is now, not later. But how could you implement this?

During your PhD you gained more skills than you thought! You can think critically, investigate problems, communicate, collaborate and master multiple technologies as well as managing projects and people. I am pretty sure you also presented or taught complex content or data sets at several levels and to diverse audiences.

The skills you feel you are lacking can be filled in by a huge amount of great (on- and offline) courses out there. Some are for free, while others come in exchange for a tiny investment. Some examples?

- If you want to build your writing skills, Nature Publishing Group offers courses called Nature Masterclasses in "Scientific Writing" as well as "Peer review and effective collaboration in research", which your present institution might have subscribed to.

- Udemy and EdX offer plenty of online classes for free on any kind of topic you could possibly think of.

- Skillshare is also a great go-to place to build a vast array of creative and soft skills.

- Codecademy courses can teach you how to proficiently master R and Python languages in science. I personally attended an R course and found it rather useful!

Tangentially related, you can also start volunteering at your institutions' postdoctoral association or other scientific career-developing groups to build new skills such as networking, communicating with new people and organizing events.

Chapter Summary: List the missing skills you might need to be successful in your new career and tailor your actions around them. Or, in other words, get yourself out there and start looking for some courses/activities that you might enjoy very much.

CHAPTER 5

Informational interviews

"I am a part of all that I have met." – Lord Tennyson

Informational interviews are very important tools in finding openings and connecting with potential employers. You can arrange interviews with people you know or with total strangers. An informational interview is an opportunity for you, the job seeker, to learn about a new career path, about an organization or a company, and about potential employment opportunities. You may have to do ten or more informational interviews before you land your first real job interview.

Everyone understands that networking is how people find jobs, and trust me – no one will be offended by your request for an informational interview, provided you follow proper etiquette. You will be amazed at how often someone will recommend you for an opportunity or introduce you to new people.

Through LinkedIn, I personally connected with great people who spared some time for me to answer questions about their transitional journey and thus created meaningful connections. I know that I will probably never meet these people in real life, but I appreciated their help and will keep in touch as things unfold (if they are happy to). This might sound awkward at first, as scientists probably aren't yet comfortable with this online way of socializing with peers and mentors. However, this is a very normal way of networking that is becoming extremely common these days.

As a rule of thumb, informational interviews help you explore a broad range of career opportunities by asking people what they actually do (something that is honestly quite hard to tell from a job title). They should be approximately 30–60 minutes long and can occur via Zoom, in person, or over the phone. A key point to remember here is the purpose of the chat: you are asking for information, not a job.

In informational interviews, it's common to ask questions about the person's career path, and it is not a good chance to ask favors. Similarly to the rules we explored for networking, always make sure to leave a positive impression.

- Tune in on time or arrive early, smile, be friendly and don't forget the eye contact.

- Break the ice with some brief small talk, but keep your intro short – in other words, don't talk about yourself for too long unless asked.

- Don't ask trivial questions that make them feel they're wasting their time and you could have just Googled their role better.

- Ask what their current role is about and how and why they transitioned.

- Ask what kinds of skills or experience they wish they'd had before job hopping.

- If you are interested in the company they work for, ask generally about their work culture.

- Always thank them for their time, and follow up with an email thanking them again.

Consider yourself a journalist for most of the interview and try to tease out information about their experience. After several interviews, you will have enough useful data to plot some sort of conclusions about (I) what job possibilities are available, (II) how you should organize your job search, (III) how to prepare for interviews and, subsequently, the negotiation process.

Do: Your homework very well. You should do enough background research before tuning in with your contact in such a way that you will demonstrate that you are a credible candidate who is committed to leaping into a new sector. Prep a brief explanation about your background and expertise and clarify what you are looking for. Follow up with a thank-you-for-your-time note. It's good manners and makes you memorable.

Don't: Go in unprepared, but instead practice informational interviews with friends and family so you get used to asking good questions and listening. Let yourself down after a negative informational interview. Ask for favors – instead, ask for advice on how to position yourself in the job market.

Need practical examples of what to ask? Have a look below, but don't ask them all at once:

- Could you describe your typical work day?

- Could you tell me a little bit about your current responsibilities?

- How did you organize your job search?

- What was your interview process like?

- What types of skills are pivotal in your position?

- What are some of the future career opportunities for someone in your position (where do you see yourself in three to five years)?

- What advice would you give to someone in my position who wants to make this transition?

By the end of your informational interview, you should have:

- Detailed information about their career journey, plus tips and tricks on how they found the position and actually succeeded as a job candidate in their interview process.

- A rough idea of what their job responsibilities and daily routine are like.

- An awareness of future career opportunities for someone in that position.

- Information about their organization's culture.

As you are approaching the end of your chat and wrapping up the meeting, you should ask for recommendations of a couple of people who would be good to talk to as you continue networking (this is a difficult one, I know – but practice and practice!). The likelihood of someone taking the time to chat with you goes up significantly if your initial request comes through a mutual contact, so it's a fast, easy way to connect and talk to even more people. Try to make this request as specific as possible, getting to the point of what kind of contacts you are looking for. Asking for instance: "Is there anyone else you would recommend speaking with in regards to opportunities in life science consulting?" will make it easier for your contact to think of someone really relevant.

Again, always follow up with a thank-you note! Even better, follow up one more time with an update on your meetings with the people they recommended and the results of your job search. Above all, your informational interviewees aren't just useful for obtaining one-time advice, but they can potentially become a long-term part of your network.

Chapter Summary: Take the time to explore informational interviews to really get intentional about your job hunt. Make sure you get the conversation going, know what you want to get out of the meeting, and don't leave without knowing whom you are contacting next.

CHAPTER 6

*Prepare your application materials
like a marketing masterpiece*

"Opportunity does not waste time with those who
are unprepared." – Idowu Koyenikan

After boring you to death with an endless list of odd-sounding job titles, I really want to make sure you don't abandon this book prematurely, so let's get to the juicy part: resume crafting. Yay!

Your resume should be all about you! It is your top marketing material as a forward-thinking and passionate professional (think about it as if you're trying to sell something) and should be tailored to your employer in order to get their attention in the top half of your page.

Components:

- Name, degree, email, phone, LinkedIn, key skills, qualifications (5–7 bullet points describing 3–5 major job requirements).

- Professional experience: describe your skills in each of the roles you worked in that are relevant to the job advertised, showing your impact and skill level in chronological order. To not be too repetitive (especially if you aren't a native English speaker) you can check 185 power verbs at muse.com.

- You can add publications, presentations, hobbies (important – they can tie back to your job, and might be a useful topic to talk about) and interests, with education at the end.

But let's take this step by step!

As a general rule, I am rather sure your resume will be scanned through hiring software called ATS (applicant tracking system), which is a scary piece of software that HR uses in order to skim the tons of applications they receive daily. If you make it through the first skimming process, you have a decent chance of making it to the hiring manager (that's the person picking up the phone and scheduling an interview with you), so attentive formatting and keywording are very important in this step.

First of all, try to remove or avoid pictures, or frankly weird elements such as italics, icons, symbols, horizontal lines, graphs (I know you would love to add some graph bars here), borders, shading and hyperlinks. These might work against you and ATS will not be able to read them.

You will probably get an immediate rejection if the file format is different from .doc or .docx. PDF will sometimes not even get through. The font size must never be below 11 points and you should be using classic styles such as Arial, Times New Roman, Verdana, etc. Don't forget to incorporate relevant keywords that align with the type of position being sought.

Before analyzing each section, let's summarize some must-have general tips for a successful resume:

- Length: 2 pages max

- Font: Arial or Times New Roman (not smaller than 11 pts) – keep it consistent!

- Not in the first person, but use adjectives to humanize the content

- Bullet points with strong action verbs (again, check muse.com)

- White spaces

- Consistent margins

- Consistent fonts

Let's step back and order the content in these sections first:

Personal Details and Professional Summary

Core Competencies and Technical Skills

Work Experience

Education

Certifications/Professional Training

Awards/Volunteer Work and Extracurricular Activities

Section 1: Personal Details And Professional Summary

This is the first part of your resume. Make sure that after your name and title you are including other relevant personal details such as email, home address, phone and LinkedIn profile. Also add your job title and related positions that you are looking into filling (just as with your LinkedIn profile) and tailor the rest of the document in harmony with these.

In the first section called "Professional Summary", you should answer the question about who you are as a person, just as when you are asked at interviews to "talk about yourself". Include adjectives like forward-thinking, dynamic, motivated, critical-thinking – and make sure to have all the verbs in present tense.

In addition, include your core competencies and transferable/ technical skills, which should be backed by quantifiable achievements. Examples of transferable skills are: leadership and management, communication and project management, team play and collaboration etc. The technical skills, on the other hand, will be more related to your specific niche of research: animal studies, western blots, rtPCR etc. You don't need to mention where exactly you developed or got these from, as these skills and achievements are transferable to other jobs.

Here is a practical example for the first part:

TIM WHITE, Ph.D. (fictional name)

twhite@gmail.com · www.linkedin.com/in/ tim-white · Location · +### ### ####

Molecular Biologist | Project Leader | R&D Scientist

Summary: Ph.D.-level multilingual scientist with expertise in XX and a broad set of skills applicable across different industries and roles. Having progressive and extensive experience in biomedical research and XX (*adapt these skills to the job description*), can craft and execute successful strategies to lead and develop projects in a fast-paced environment. Resilient, flexible and adaptable achiever with keen attention to detail.

CORE COMPETENCIES AND TECHNICAL SKILLS

Leadership and Management. Developed leadership skills in managing technicians, mentoring Masters students (XX) and pre-doc fellows (XX), overseeing projects from planning through execution, troubleshooting and publication.

Communication. Effective communicator across all levels of the organization, able to prepare diverse global presentations with cultural sensitivity and emotional intelligence. Fluent in French and English; proficient in German.

Creativity and Innovation. Proactively generated, brainstormed, and implemented unique ideas/solutions for problem-solving at a competitive edge, which translated into $XXk of new funding for research budget.

Project Management. Developed a track record of independent critical thinking, excellent teamwork and scientific achievement, demonstrated by X international presentations and XX publications in top-tier, high-impact journals such as XX.

Technical Skills. · Molecular biology: DNA/RNA extraction, cloning, overexpression and knockdown of genes, PCR. · Mammalian cell culture: · Animal studies: genetically engineering, breeding, and maintaining transgenic mouse models. · Computer skills: Adobe Creative Suite (Photoshop, Illustrator, Lightroom), Python, R, Graphpad Prism, Wave (Agilent), Image J, Mendely, Endnote, Microsoft Office (Word, Excel, PowerPoint).

Section 2: Achievements, Or Main Body

Verbs should turn to the past tense now, as you are showing compelling evidence of how your actions led to results in your past experience. You are also showcasing your problem-solving skills and how you can contribute to the company in the future. In other words, you should try to define the challenges you faced and briefly describe the actions you took to solve these problems. Also describe (possibly quantifying in numbers) how your employer or company benefited from the outcome. What were your top 3–5 contributions in each role?

As a simple storytelling reference, break down your experience in such a way:

- Situation

- Action

- Results

- Learning

An easy example could be: Shadowed junior Masters student by incorporating rotation of training programs, which resulted in 3 excellent Masters thesis and 2 publications.

In addition, don't be scared of sharing examples of projects that failed or didn't go exactly the way you wanted them to.

Section 2 template:

WORK EXPERIENCE

Cornell University, New York, USA. May 2019 – Present

Research Scientist

- Genetically engineered XX tissue specific (Crispr/Cas9 and AAV vectors) transgenic mouse models involved in cancer metabolism, optimized several *in vivo* and *in vitro* assays to discern deep molecular mechanisms.

- Worked with colleagues to discover new druggable targets: conducted screening of >400.000 compounds, developed functional assays and optimization.

- Demonstrated ability to optimize assays and work independently that led to submission of 1 patent for a novel ELISA system aimed at industrial manufacturing.

University of Oxford, Oxford, UK. Feb 2017 – Mar 2019

Postdoctoral Scientist and Lecturer

- Led and operated *in vivo* studies to evaluate therapeutic effect of XX inhibition in genetic and xenobiotic disease models in the field of XX.

- Gained further experience with cell-based assays and associated molecular techniques (e.g. ChIP, flow cytometry, plasmid transfection).

- Ideated/created lessons and remodelled projects to contribute to the curriculum of PhD students.

University of Oxford, Oxford, UK. Aug 2015 – Nov 2016

Research Assistant

- Conducted and perfected molecular biology techniques such as RT-PCR, cell culture, flow cytometry, ELISA and Western blot aimed at assessing early immunodeficiencies in pediatric patients.

Section 3: Education, Volunteer Work And Publications

In the "Education" section you should add the title of your studies and degree in bold, whereas the name of the university should be in plain characters. You can decide to include salient keywords for your thesis or degree program that might feel interesting and within scope. Afterwards, you can also include a section on certification and professional training if relevant to the job post. And another one with volunteer work or awards, publications and relevant patents. Don't make this too lengthy – remember that your resume should still fit within a maximum of two pages, so especially if you're an experienced researcher I wouldn't list all your publications (but rather quantify them or link to your PubMed).

Example for Section 3:

EDUCATION (feel free to include thesis keywords)

PhD: Microbiology. Cornell University, NY, USA. 2013 – 2017

Master of Science: Molecular Biology. UCLA, LA, USA. 2009 – 2011

Bachelor of Science: Biology. University of Padua, Italy. 2005 – 2009

VOLUNTEER WORK

Science Communicator @ScienceIG: Developed a Science Communication platform on Instagram to explain complicated technologies to a broader audience.

Community Volunteer, No Hunger program. Served at weekly kitchen services.

Postdoctoral Association, Event Manager. Facilitated the connection of international scientists through career-development events and networking opportunities in the NYC area.

I would recommend you to save this as a master resume, which you only need to tailor slightly each time according to the job description. An easy way to do this is to scan the job post for keywords by copying and pasting the job description into a word cloud software (such as https://tagcrowd.com/). Do the same with your resume, keeping the result on a separate tab, and finally try to visualize what keywords are missing that can be implemented to make you a top candidate.

Tailor your resume for each job. It must be clear from the beginning how you are adding value to the position! This is your sell sheet, so make it obvious that you spent time studying the job description.

Cover Letter

The main aspects of a successful and well-written cover letter are:

- Always cross-reference the core competencies and achievements of your resume with the job requirements, demonstrating how you add value and meet the job requirements

- Think about what you've done in the past and how you can transfer this in the future

- Think again about the "tell me a bit about yourself" question and align the content of your cover letter with the opening paragraph of your resume

- Do thorough research on the company and answer the question: "why do you want to work for us?"

Frame your letter in such a way:

1. Name of hiring manager, recruiter etc. Dept. name.

     Company name.
2. Paragraph 1: Which role you are applying for, the "what" you are professionally with the "who" you are in terms of personal attributes, both of which make you a suitable candidate for the role.
3. Paragraph 2: Cross-reference the "Core Competencies and Technical Skills" section of your resume to answer the job requirements, e.g. which skills and achievements do you have that prove you are able to perform this role?
4. Paragraph 3: Mention three facts about the company and why they appeal to you. State how you will add value to the organization.
5. Paragraph 4: Thank the reader for his/her time and state that you are attaching your resume for their consideration.
6. Sign off: Name, phone number, email and LinkedIn URL.

A cover letter must be one page long, while if you decide to embed this into an email, try to stick to a maximum of 400 words (longer emails are hard to read). Attach your resume only for their review.

A template for a cover letter can be as following:

Date <>

Location <>

Dear <Hiring Manager's name>,

I am writing regarding your present job opening of <role> as advertised on <website>.

As a candidate with extensive experience in <your main topic>, I am highly skilled in <your key technical skills which are relevant to the job post>, as previously performed in <give an example referring to your past experience and cross-linking to your CV>.

My solid international background has allowed me to <mention soft and transferable skills linked to the job post, e.g. work with teams with exceptional performance, deliver a high standard of scientific achievement>.

The opportunity to join <company> greatly interests me because I truly believe <add company values e.g. in the company culture as a chance to make a positive impact on people's lives> and I foresee great possibility to grow/thrive within it.

As a holder of <education, e.g. a PhD from Weill Cornell Medicine>, I can <list hard skills required, e.g. competently execute, plan and document experiments and techniques in a team, as I am eager to work within a group of diverse professionals.>

<closing sentence> I believe that I would make a valuable asset to <your team or company> and I hereby offer my resume for your review.

<thank them for their time> Thank you in advance for your time and consideration. I look forward to hearing from you at your earliest convenience.

Best regards,

<your name>

<phone number>

<email><LinkedIn>

Before clicking that "submit your application" button

Now that you have all your marketing materials ready, it's time to use them for the best results! Before clicking the submit button, make absolutely sure that:

1. You read the job listing at least twice and adapted everything accordingly

2. You utilized the website jobscan.co to compare your resume to the job listing you provided (their motto is "Get past resume robots"). Once you get the estimated score, this should be an 80% or higher match before you submit your application to the company for consideration. To improve your score, go back and revise the other highlighted words that were similar to the ones used by the job listing.

3. The spelling is checked very well each time you adapt your documents to new postings.

4. You aren't overstuffing your resume with keywords. It will hurt you in the long run if the document itself is just a wordy list that doesn't make a lot of sense.

5. You aren't lying on your resume or cover letter.

How Do You Stand Out With Your Job Application Material?

Hiring managers receive thousands of networking requests and hundreds of unsolicited resumes every day. How are you going to ensure that you stand out?

- Do your homework – show that you have taken the time to understand the organization as well as your contact's background. It's even better if you can contribute a suggestion or new perspective on business challenges they are facing.

- Be unique with your outreach medium – as I said, they do get tons of networking requests and resumes. Try to be original about it! For instance, a connection recently sent me a tailored voice message wishing me happy holidays and asking how I was doing. I found that quite a unique approach.

When you need to differentiate yourself from the crowds, think as yourself being literally like a product – branding, marketing and selling yourself effectively by:
- Defining your personal brand
- Understanding the market needs (running a thorough external analysis to understand your specific industry niche, the organization itself and its culture)
- Developing your marketing plan: getting really clear about what to focus your search on and which type of company you'd prefer to target, optimizing your resume and networking skills.
- Delivering your message clearly, practicing interviews and behavioral questions, and strategizing your content.

Here is a scheme that might help you with memorizing that:

Once you're confident in standing out with your marketing materials, where will you find opportunities? Look on the company website, Indeed, Simplyhired, Higheredjobs, LinkedIn nature science and your network. Flexjobs also is interesting for part-time remote jobs.

Application process: As diverse as the career options are within the pharmaceutical and biotechnology industries, the application process is surprisingly similar and streamlined.

Larger companies will have a "Careers" section on their website in which you can search the openings that are publicly listed. Of course, don't let that stop you from contacting someone directly to express your interest via an informational interview. Although it's easy to go through the process of submitting your resume and application online, beware that you will be subject to the computerized world that will screen out applications lacking the keywords mentioned in the qualifications section of the listing. You should do your best to make sure that the materials and information that you are submitting will not immediately take you out of the running for an interview.

For start-ups, this process might be less computerized and more personal. You will normally be asked to send an email with your application material to a real person! This means you will actually need to craft an email aimed at capturing their attention and tailor your cover letter and resume accordingly.

Chapter Summary: Craft lean, impactful and concise application materials, checking for spelling mistakes and adapting them slightly each time in order to satisfy the specific requirements of each job. Stand out from the crowd by defining your brand, understanding the market's demands, and tailoring your message to your future employer.

CHAPTER 7

Interviews: No nerdy T-shirts, dress for success!

"Anyone who has never made a mistake has never tried anything new." – Albert Einstein

Getting an interview means the employer sees you as a qualified candidate and is interested in hearing more about your training, skills and experience. This is a very good result, as it proves that all the marketing materials you learned about in the previous pages actually work!

You should look closely into the prospective companies you are interviewing with and pinpoint four things about them that really appeal to you. Now you should ask yourself: How do I add value? What is it about me that gives the company value?

According to Corralling Chaos, a human resources consultancy, one of the most important key qualities assessed during an interview is trust. And this cannot be understood simply by reading your resume. Trust is made up of ability (soft and hard skills), good intent and benevolence (behavior), integrity (cultural and character – enthusiastic, reliable, calm, fun..).

In order to convey trust, succeed at interviews and have a pleasant experience, prepare effectively and look your best. It is well proven that it takes just a few seconds to make a first impression – in fact, in this very brief time people will decide whether they like and trust you (and this applies to networking too).

It is pivotal at this point to build confidence and warmth by:

- Preparing your story very well for when someone asks you the "tell me a bit about yourself" question.

- Never speaking badly about your former employer when you are asked why you left your past role (for example, mention that you are seeking a different challenge with more career growth, more responsibility, etc.).

- Having a clear theme and storyline, implemented with vivid language and confident presentation – tone, for instance, is important here, as well as speed and articulation (you want to sound genuine, and don't want to pack too much information in at one time).

- Showing competence: you know a lot about the company and you are credible!

- Improving your body language (most of a message's meaning comes across through your non-verbal communication):

+ Keep eye contact

+ Have a genuine smile

+ Hold a nice posture (do this on the phone too), showing enthusiasm

+ Raise your chin

+ Keep your gestures open (even if you have a phone or video interview, this will change your tone of voice and give it authenticity)

+ Slightly lean forward to communicate interest

The power of storytelling

When you're in a job interview and are asked questions such as "give me an example of how you dealt with a difficult situation at your previous job", the hiring manager is aiming to understand what transferable skills you have (and find out those personality traits we mentioned in Chapter 4). The answer can't simply be "I used my great teamwork skills and emotional communication", as this has no meaning whatsoever! You will need to come up with and craft a compelling story around what happened.

As a matter of fact, all stories share a known framework:

1. Beginning (challenges you faced)
2. Middle (what you did, actions taken, troubleshooting)
3. End (what the outcome was)

If you train yourself to see your work challenges through this framework, it becomes much easier to answer such questions. Get better at this by practicing in everyday life with friends or colleagues, so as to get more objective feedback. Plan your storytelling around the most in-demand soft skills!

According to polls by famous job-hunting platforms such as Indeed and Monster, the following remain the most sought-after skills that employers look for in interviews:

- Collaboration – teamwork, conflict management

- Adaptability – being resourceful, versatile, flexible

- Leadership – how you are proactive, eager, solution-oriented, take initiative

- Growth potential – your aspirations, ambitions and goals, learning attitude, upscaling

- Prioritization – organization, and time and resources management

- Culture Add – your passions or what you do outside work (read about people who work at the company and try to understand what they do)

When you have this list in mind, you can leverage your professional story around it and build a reference file with examples for each of the above.

Hays, a leading global recruitment company, elegantly summed up[11] a few points on how to prepare your mindset before entering that interview room or picking up a call:

Adopt a positive and constructive mindset: a positive frame of mind will enable you to perform at your very best during the interview, in the knowledge that you are as prepared as possible. It will also help you feel more confident, helping you to really sell yourself and your skills to the interviewer in an authentic way , even if you are doing so remotely (via phone or Zoom). Needless to say, with a positive mindset in place, you will also be able to enjoy your interview more and portray your authentic self from start to finish – a person who is confident, articulate and fully deserving of this wonderful opportunity. Ultimately, that is who you are! So don't doubt for a single moment that you are anything else than that.

Approach this interview as a great opportunity for growth, and feel excited. Whether the interview is a success or a total disaster, whether it goes the way you want or not, you can be sure to learn something from it. At the end of the day, a job interview is a great opportunity to be introduced to new people and could open many new doors to ultimately landing the next exciting step in your career. I know it's not always easy to see things through a positive filter, especially if you have been outside the job market for a long time, but try your best to use this chance as a great learning opportunity. For instance, you might figure out new opportunities, or get a better sense of what you want and don't want from your career, and where your present strengths and weaknesses lie. Constructive feedback from your interviewer after a rejection might also shed light on what you need to focus on next to get ahead in your career. These are priceless outcomes that you can leverage for the rest of your job hunt. In addition, the more experience you gain, the better you will get at interviewing, becoming a more self-confident and well-rounded professional. So, even if you don't get the job, you will still gain knowledge and more experience, which is certainly not a bad thing. Focus on the journey and not the destination, they say!

Don't let imposter syndrome kick in. In other words, cage those confidence gremlins and keep them where they are! This is a huge part of your positive mindset, so remind yourself often of your worth, taking this self-belief into your job interview instead of thinking "everyone is going to be better than me". As I mentioned earlier, many people suffer from something called imposter syndrome, which is defined by the website Verywell Mind as: "an internal experience of believing that you are not as competent as others perceive you to be"[12]. Essentially, this is the feeling that you are fooling others into thinking you're better at something, or more capable, than you really are, and that you do not deserve the success you have experienced so far. It's likely that imposter syndrome is what's making you feel like you perhaps aren't good enough for this interview, or that your success so far hasn't been real. This might be making it more difficult to remember all the things you have achieved so far. But it's so important you turn this limiting mindset away by telling yourself that your success is ultimately down to your own competence and effort, not luck. And even if your current responsibilities look a little different, all those skills and experiences you have built up still exist and are still part of your capabilities.

Take a break. Don't focus too much on your career! Yes, it's important to prepare well for any job interview, but even when an interview is coming, don't forget to find time to enjoy activities away from work. So, keep on investing time in friendships, and any hobbies or interests that will eventually help you to keep focused on your career path and blow off some steam from time to time. In other words, get some quality sleep, meet and chat with friends and family, exercise, have a healthy diet, get out and enjoy nature. You should keep this up and running with your daily job-seeking routine.

Pick the right outfit for the interview. Even if this is a video or telephone interview, it is still imperative you dress as if you were meeting the interviewer face to face. I know you would love to wear just a shirt and underwear (since you're video-calling) or your favorite ThermoFisher Scientific T-shirt/hoodie. However, dressing sharply and in tune with the position for which you are applying will help you to feel self-assured on this very important occasion. In fact, the smallest touches do make a difference! Wearing your best shoes and trousers, despite the fact they will probably not be seen, will nurture a positive mindset ahead of and during the actual interview. Depending on the company, whether it's a small start-up or a big player in your field, dress casual/modern and professional: it's up to you if you decide to bring in color (there are plenty of studies out there analyzing the psychology behind it), calibrating and thinking carefully about it, as what you wear says a lot about yourself.

Sample questions

Behavioral interviewing is often used by hiring managers to get to know more about your skills and expertise and how they fit the job. These are some sample questions you could work on according to agilent careers (I recommend you prepare post-its and play mock-interviewing with a friend):

- **Describe a situation that required you to make a prompt decision.** What factors did you consider? How did you assess the risks involved? How comfortably did you proceed with making a decision?

- **Give an example of a situation where you had to take initiative.** Why was this necessary? How did you feel about the initiative taken and what would you do differently next time?

- **Share an example of when you had to take responsibility for**

a project or a group of people. What did you do? What was particularly successful and/or less successful than expected?

- Describe a situation where it was important that you identified and understood the needs of others. How did you engage and communicate with those involved? What was the outcome?

- Tell me about a time when you had to adapt your own style to work well with others in a team. How did you approach this? What did you do to build team spirit and what was the outcome?

Chapter Summary: Be positive and honest, prepare your story (research and practice), highlight skills and experience. Remember, this is not an exam or a criminal interrogation, but just a professional conversation! So to keep it that way, try to steer away from politics and frankly avoid comments on beliefs or religion. As a good sign that you did your homework, take a notebook with you and be prepared to ask what the next steps are, thanking them for their time at the end of the chat.

CHAPTER 8

Negotiating towards a final offer

"Don't bargain yourself down before you get
to the table." – Carol Frohlinger

When your round of interviews is approaching its end, and you've managed to convey a great impression of yourself, you will typically get to the scary question:

"if we were to move forward with the job offer, what would be your salary requirements?"

Now, this is a really tricky one. Nobody likes asking for money, or sometimes even talking about it! Just FYI: the person you are talking to already has a range of payment in mind for each position. They come to that by benchmarking surveys within the biotech market, for instance, so they will try to keep the offer within this range.

If you don't have an actual number in mind, your initial response should be:

"I'm very interested in this position, and I very much hope that an offer will be made with a salary that is competitive for my background and experience."

Often it happens that the hiring manager will ask you again to come up with a number. A good strategy may be: instead of looking this up on Glassdoor or other salary websites, reach out to connections that have (or had) a similar role, ask what a competitive compensation is like and use that as a benchmark.

As a rule, I would let them come up with and "anchor" a number first! Neither side has perfect information when they get to the interview table, meaning that you might not have the confidence to leverage your position in your favour. By letting them start, you might get lucky or not, but at least you have a starting point! The last thing you want to get out of this conversation is that gut-wrenching feeling of being treated unfairly or getting underpaid.

Finally, if you really have to come up with a number, use a range like $90k to $110k per year or, if you are prompted for a single figure, always use an odd one! Studies show that odd numbers sound more immovable, serious and better thought-through than round ones (which are temporary placeholders).

A brief note: I know, getting a job offer feels amazing! But remember, you have to patiently evaluate what they are offering, whether you really want the job, and then negotiate to get what you are happy with – or instead make the decision to turn it down. If the offer and terms of work don't feel like you and aren't what you need, walking away is the right choice!

In this phase of your job-seeking process, becoming a proficient negotiator is essential in order for you to get what you want from the conversation. To gain more insights into this topic, I attended a great hands-on seminar by Sam Swift, who is Head of Data & AI at Bowery and holds a PhD in behavioral economics.

I got to brainstorm, think and nail down my so-called BATNA first. BATNA is the Best Alternative to a Negotiated Agreement, meaning a description of what you will do if you cannot reach an agreement. The negotiation starts with the realization that what you are asking doesn't align with what the person on the other side wants, and you will have to find a Zone of Possible Agreement (ZOPA) with them. This is the in-between zone that shares a portion of what you are asking and what they can offer you. As an example, you are looking into a yearly compensation of $90k to $110k for a Senior Scientist role, whereas the hiring manager wants to close the deal at $80k to $97k. The ZOPA will be between $90k and $97k, and this will be the range you can negotiate your salary within.

Generally speaking, your tactic should unfold as follows:

1. Plan your BATNA, understand their ZOPA, and target accordingly!
2. Make the opening offer if you have enough information.
3. Craft a specific offer and be intentional about it, but be open to playing by ear.

It's a good idea to try to articulate your requests in a multi-issue fashion, focusing firstly on interests and not the position itself. You should always trade your biggest issues for theirs (balancing value-claiming and value-creating) by learning about your counterpart while teaching them about you. But let's expand on this in more detail.

If your interview goes well, you will receive an offer letter, which you need to read very carefully to understand what is negotiable and what is not. You definitely want to make sure that your worth is well recognized by your prospective employer.

The negotiation process might seem difficult – nobody wants to do it! But life is all about negotiations, and I would recommend you to get better at it! I found the book *Never Split the Difference: Negotiating As If Your Life Depended On It* by Christopher Voss and Tahl Raz really helpful, in which a former FBI agent explains some tips and tricks for how to negotiate in everyday life.

So, how do you ask for things that you want or need while

maintaining a good relationship? As you will typically be negotiating with either a hiring manager or your future boss, what is the best way to ask?

Prepare very well for the conversation first:

1. Revise the job offer.
2. Prioritize questions and requests, and divide them into must-have items and nice-to-have items.
3. Based on the latter, write down your discussion bullets on what is most important for you to request.
4. Practice this scenario out loud with a partner in a mock interview setting.

Decide if you want the job and be really clear about your must-haves and good-to-haves! Be confident – it's OK to negotiate, everyone does it!

What is normally acceptable to negotiate?

- Title and position (e.g.. Scientist I or Senior Scientist depending on your experience)

- Relocation package

- Start date

- Bonus

- Stock options (more common in start-ups)

What is normally seen as non negotiable? (This is often country-dependent)

- Vacation time (number of holidays per year)

- Healthcare plans

- Retirement plan

Now that you know what is negotiable and what isn't, let's guide you through how to ask for what you want:

1. Start very positively, stating clearly that you like the company very much and that you are excited about joining it.
2. Transition to your prepared agenda, stating for instance that you would like to discuss three important points.
3. If you want to negotiate your salary, try to leverage your position by, for instance, mentioning another competing job offer to make the current offer more appealing. You can also come up with statistics or anecdotes from other scientists who have worked in this position.
4. If you don't have data you can still ask for something more, coming up with your needs based on facts (e.g. that you would need a car to commute).
5. Always remember at this point that the company wants you.

Once the conversation ends, finish up with an encouraging tone and verbally summarize your understanding. It's always good practice to follow up with an email expressing your appreciation!

Always negotiate with integrity, and maintain a good relationship by showing appreciation at the beginning and end of each conversation.

Chapter Summary: Do not accept the first offer that is given to you – this might be significantly lower than what the company is willing to pay you. So do your research and discover what is an appropriate salary for the position. Stick to that number and focus on the value you will bring to the company.

FINAL REMARKS AND TAKE-HOME MESSAGE

"There is no real ending. It's just the place where you stop the story." – Frank Herbert

As we read throughout these pages, the job search for PhDs wanting to make the leap into the private sector is tortuous and at times slippery. It starts well before applying for a job or contacting a potential employer, but this preparation phase makes it interesting, fun and eventually successful.

We've learned how to craft personal storytelling materials such as a resume, cover letter and solid online presence. As you leap upstream along your career river, keep this important advice in mind and learn how to put it into practice in your everyday life. I bet that by now you can master them all – as a PhD you are definitely a great achiever and learner. You've made it through your career journey this far, and although this unprecedented path will take you to waters you've never swum in before, you should approach the journey with positivity and mindfulness.

We as academics have a full truck of soft and hard skills to offer! They're already a part of us: we've been building them all the way till now, so we just need to get better at showing them to the external world.

This journey is your own, so make it worthwhile and enjoy the process of getting there! And don't forget to share it with colleagues and loved ones, which makes it so much more interesting and rewarding.

To close, this from a real scientist: further research is needed! And surely more work needs to be done at our end to explore this topic deeper and open new avenues. Remember, we aren't alone in this – plenty of other people were once in the same situation and managed it successfully! And now they are out there, willing and super happy to help!

So: stay motivated, reach out, and work towards making a great leap!

About The Author

Matteo Tardelli, PhD is currently based in New York, and works as a Postdoctoral Scientist at Weill Cornell Medicine. He is an avid traveller and has gained diverse experience in industry and academia around the globe (Italy, UK, Austria and USA). Matteo is the author of 18+ original scientific publications, which have appeared in respected scientific journals by Elselvier, Nature and Wiley.

After many years in academia, he decided to explore different paths away from tenure-track positions and added to what he learned by speaking with experts and career coaches.

Matteo defines himself as "just another salmon swimming upstream". In fact, he strongly believes that sharing his journey with peers is a unique approach to bringing value to the PhD community, and making academics more appreciated and employable in the future.

His first non-academic publication, *The Salmon Leap for PhDs*, aims at being exactly this peer-to-peer toolkit, made up of clear and actionable advice for colleagues.

To date, aside from doing science, he has assisted many researchers in gaining the confidence to launch new and diverse careers by taking part in career panels, and volunteering for scientific communities such as postdoctoral associations and networking societies.

References

1. Globalization and Its Impacts on the Quality of PhD Education. Forces and Forms in Doctoral Education Worldwide. Editors: Nerad, Maresi, Evans, Barbara (Eds.); Springer, 2014.
2. https://www.werenotreallystrangers.com/.
3. *The Squiggly Career* by Helen Tupper and Sarah Ellis. 2020.
4. PhDs: the tortuous truth. https://www.nature.com/articles/d41586-019-03459-7; Chris Woolston; Nature, 2019.
5. The 7 Characteristics of a Great Networker. https://www.entrepreneur.com/article/302631; Ivan Misner, 2017.
6. Things You Probably Didn't Know About Your Job Search. https://www.forbes.com/sites/jacquelynsmith/2013/04/17/7-things-you-probably-didnt-know-about-your-job-search/#759d7c638110; Jacquelyn Smith, Forbes 2013.
7. What Is the Hidden Job Market? https://www.thebalancecareers.com/what-is-the-hidden-job-market-2062004; Alison Doyle, 2020.
8. Career Exploration -- A Grand Experiment. https://www.insidehighered.com/advice/2020/04/27/scientific-way-phd-students-can-frame-their-career-explorations-opinion; Briana Konnick, Inside HigherEd, 2020.
9. *Working Identity - Nine Unconventional Strategies For Reinventing Your Career,* Herminia Ibarra, Harvard Business School Press 2003.
10. NPA Core Competencies, https://www.nationalpostdoc.org/page/CoreCompetencies
11. 10 ways to get into a positive

mindset before your remote job interview. https://social.hays.com/2020/04/03/positive-mindset-before-remote-job-interview/; Marc Burrage, 2020.

12. What Is Imposter Syndrome? https://www.verywellmind.com/imposter-syndrome-and-social-anxiety-disorder-4156469; Arlin Cuncic, 2020.

Additional Resources And People To Follow

People to follow on social media:

Tracy Costello, PhD is a dedicated career coach who frequently hosts online training sessions especially tailored to postdocs. She is a member of the Board of Directors at the National Postdoctoral Association and Executive Coach at STEMpeers, so she is definitely a great go-to expert. https://www.linkedin.com/in/tracycostello/

Joanne Kamens, PhD is Executive Director at Addgene, a non-profit dedicated to facilitating collaboration and material-sharing in the scientific community. https://www.linkedin.com/in/joannekamens/

Karin Bodewits is the founder of NaturalScience.Careers and an author and speaker, publishing articles around the topics "women and career" and "academic life". https://www.linkedin.com/in/karin-bodewits-771a908/

Kirsty Bonner is a career advisor, also hosting frequent webinars on career development https://www.linkedin.com/in/kirsty-bonner/

Madeline Mann is a talent development and human resources professional, who posts very useful tips with a fresh millennial touch. https://www.linkedin.com/in/madelinemann/

Diana YK Chang is a career coach who helps her clients to become more marketable. https://mymarketability.com/

Brenda Meller helps people and companies unlock the power of LinkedIn. https://www.linkedin.com/in/brendameller/

Associations to join or follow:

Cheeky Scientist: https://cheekyscientist.com/

National Postdoctoral Association: https://www.nationalpostdoc.org/

Smart Tribe: https://smarttribe.io/

Career development websites:

NIH office of intramural training & education: https://www.training.nih.gov/

Next Scientist: https://www.nextscientist.com/

Biomed Badass: https://biomedbadass.com/

The Muse: https://www.themuse.com/

Inside Higher Ed: https://insidehighered.com/

The Chronicle of Higher Education: https://www.chronicle.com/?cid=UCHETOPNAV

Postdoc In USA: https://postdocinusa.com/

SciPhD: https://sciphd.com/

Addgene blog: https://blog.addgene.org/

Rutgers iJOB: http://rubest.rutgers.edu/

Vitae: https://www.vitae.ac.uk/

Books to read or listen to:

The PhD Career Coaching Guide by Tina Persson (2020)

Next Gen PhD by Melanie V. Sinche (2016)

Changing Hats: A book for academics looking beyond academia by Daria Gritsenko (2017)

The Portable PhD: Taking Your Psychology Career Beyond Academia by M. Patrick Gallagher, Ashleigh Gallagher (2020)

The Squiggly Career by Helen Tupper and Sarah Ellis. (2020)

Never Split the Difference: Negotiating As If Your Life Depended On It by Christopher Voss and Tahl Raz (2016)

What Color Is Your Parachute? 2020: A Practical Manual for Job-Hunters and Career-Changers by Richard N. Bolles (2019)

www.ingramcontent.com/pod-product-compliance
Lightning Source LLC
Chambersburg PA
CBHW070119230526
45472CB00004B/1331